fantastic
STASH QUILTS

8 Projects 2 Ways Using Yardage or Scraps

Joyce Dean Gieszler

KANSAS CITY
STAR QUILTS
an imprint of C&T Publishing

Text copyright © 2016 by Joyce Dean Gieszler

Photography and artwork copyright © 2016 by C&T Publishing, Inc.

Publisher: Amy Marson

Creative Director: Gailen Runge

Editors: Karla Menaugh and Liz Aneloski

Technical Editors: Nan Powell and Debbie Rodgers

Cover/Book Design: Page + Pixel

Production Coordinators: Tim Manibusan and Zinnia Heinzmann

Production Editors: Jennifer Warren and Nicole Rolandelli

Illustrator: Kirstie L. Pettersen

Photo Assistant: Carly Jean Marin

Instructional photography by Diane Pedersen, unless otherwise noted

Published by Kansas City Star Quilts, an imprint of C&T Publishing, Inc., P.O. Box 1456, Lafayette, CA 94549

Library of Congress Cataloging-in-Publication Data

Names: Gieszler, Joyce Dean, 1957- author.

Title: Fantastic stash quilts : 8 projects 2 ways using yardage or scraps / Joyce Dean Gieszler.

Description: Lafayette, CA : C&T Publishing, Inc., [2016]

Identifiers: LCCN 2016009735 | ISBN 9781617453380 (soft cover)

Subjects: LCSH: Patchwork quilts. | Patchwork--Patterns.

Classification: LCC TT835 .G534 2016 | DDC 746.46--dc23

LC record available at https://lccn.loc.gov/2016009735

Printed in China

10 9 8 7 6 5 4 3 2 1

Dedication

This, my second book, is dedicated to my students and every person who has ever attended one of my lectures. Every time that I teach or speak, I learn something as well. I can't begin to list everything I've learned from the students I've taught—sometimes it is a new ruler, tool, or technique; better time management; color combinations I would never have tried; new blogs to visit; or yet another way to make half-square triangles. Sometimes it is a comment made after a lecture that touches me. I am continually awed by what a loving, caring community we have in quilters. Need something? Just ask a quilter. Better yet, ask one of my students!

Acknowledgments

There's such a large cast to thank that I feel like someone may usher me off stage before I get finished! Don't let anyone try to fool you—the supporting cast and crew are the reason all the work gets done! I'd like to thank my mother for my love of sewing, my family for supporting my endeavors, and my group of quilting friends for their encouragement and help. I'd also like to thank my pattern testers and my binding experts.

When friends found out about my second book, they came out in great numbers to help. All of the following deserve awards for helping me make this book a reality: Betsy Biller, Karla Brokaw, AnnMarie Cowley, Donna Duckett, Cheryl Ferris, Annette Mandel, LoisMarie Mayer, Anna Munsey, Donna Pastori, Muriel Peterson, Leanne Reid, Cathie Smith, Marge York, and Christine Young.

My team at C&T made writing a book with a new publisher much easier than I'd imagined it would be. In order of appearance, my thanks go to Roxane Cerda, Karla Menaugh, Nan Powell, Kristy Zacharias, Carly Jean Marin, Zinnia Heinzmann, Jennifer Warren, and the host of others who participated. C&T truly is a family and I'm proud to be part of it!

Table of Contents

Introduction

I was very surprised last year when a student said, "I signed up for your class, but I don't do scrappy. What else have you got?" This question, probably more than most factors, led me to design patterns in two options—one scrappy version and one controlled version. Sometimes just the coloration changed, and sometimes the look of the quilt changed completely. At the same time, my fabric collection reached proportions that started weighing on me, and I knew it was time to make quilts by shopping at home first.

My fabric stash is a little like abstract art—it always makes me *feel* something! When looking through my stash, I alternately feel awe, shock, embarrassment, thrill, bafflement, love, dismay, and many more emotions.

Some of my earliest memories are of shopping with my mother and touching fabric to make sure it was of good quality. I feel closest to my mother in a fabric store. While I could use that as an excuse, I don't really have one for amassing a large collection of fabric. I just love it all! Sometimes I buy three yards of a fabric, thinking it would make a great border on a large quilt. Sometimes I buy just one yard each of several fabrics because I love them so much, even though I don't have a plan in mind. Last year I started working on a quilt with tiny 3″ stars made with Civil War–era reproduction fabric. A friend and I both thought the quilt would look good if I used a "dirty pink" fabric for alternate blocks. Since I was making a large quilt, I calculated I would need five yards of this pink. I am now the proud owner of more than twenty yards of pink fabric—none of which works for this project! It turns out that the project looks better with blue. (Yes, I just designed a new quilt starting with the pink I already had on hand.)

I also have to admit that I sometimes buy fabric by the bolt! Yes, the bolt. Sometimes I share the fabric with a friend, but at other times I just want to keep the fabric on hand—a great white background, a favorite gray, anything that I know will work with a lot of patterns. You'll see throughout the book that I have used a lot of white backgrounds.

Many of the patterns in this book began their lives as line drawings of quilts. I love looking at the lines of a quilt drawing to see the possibilities in the design before I start thinking about colors. The line drawing lets me look at the flow of the design. That, in turn, frees me up to think about color. To plan my quilt colors, I color in the line drawings just as you would color in a page in a coloring book. Frequently I have a color scheme in mind, such as the black, blue, red, pink, and cream in *Chain and Bar* (page 18). I didn't know how well the colors would play together or which would look best next to each other—I just knew that I loved them all and wanted them in a quilt together. I have included a line drawing with each pattern so that you can test the colors for yourself. Maybe you'll even find a new design within the interplay of the blocks!

Some of the instructions in this book are written for the scrappy version and some for the controlled version. All of the projects contain the yardage for both options (separately if they vary), so it will be easy to shop your stash for new projects. Mind you, I sometimes bought new fabric to freshen a quilt or the stash, but most of these quilts came right out of my fabric closet. I hope you enjoy my experiments in color and design as much as I did!

Projects

Betsy's Quilt

Finished unit: 4″ × 4″ • Finished quilt: 64½″ × 64½″

Betsy's Quilt, 64½″ × 64½″, made by Joyce Dean Gieszler, quilted by Cheryl Ferris, 2014

Materials

The feature project uses yardage for a consistent colorway. For a scrappy version, see Betsy's Scrappy Quilt *(page 11).*

PINK ¾ yard (includes binding)

PURPLE ½ yard

BLUE ½ yard

GREEN ⅞ yard

YELLOW ½ yard

RED 1⅓ yards

ORANGE ⅝ yard

WHITE 1⅞ yards

BACKING: 4 yards

BATTING: 72″ × 72″

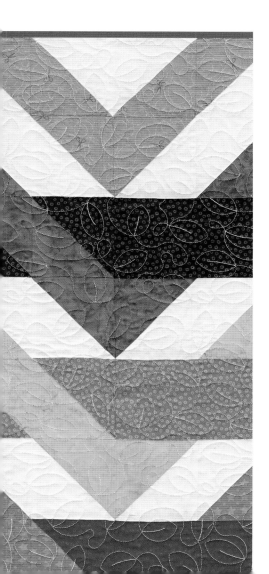

This project actually named itself. My friend Betsy loved it so much that she tested the pattern before it was even written. She had a chart with cutting instructions and some very general sewing instructions, and off she went. Betsy's longarm quilter loved the quilt so much that she posted it on her blog with the title "Betsy's quilt." Unfortunately for me, the longarm quilter lives in my area, and I had planned to use this pattern as a mystery quilt for a class for my local guild. I ended up waiting nearly three years to use this quilt for the mystery class in case anyone had seen it online!

Cutting

PINK

- Cut 1 strip 5″ × the width of fabric.
  Subcut 6 squares 5″ × 5″.
- Cut 7 strips 2¼″ × the width of fabric for the binding.

PURPLE

- Cut 1 strip 5″ × the width of fabric.
  Subcut 4 squares 5″ × 5″.
  From the remainder of the strip, cut 1 rectangle 4½″ × 12½″.
- Cut 1 strip 4½″ × the width of fabric.
  Subcut 3 rectangles 4½″ × 12½″.

BLUE

- Cut 2 strips 5″ × the width of fabric.
  Subcut 10 squares 5″ × 5″.

GREEN

- Cut 1 strip 5″ × the width of fabric.
  Subcut 8 squares 5″ × 5″.
- Cut 4 strips 4½″ × the width of fabric.
  Subcut 4 rectangles 4½″ × 20½″.

YELLOW

- Cut 2 strips 5″ × the width of fabric.
  Subcut 16 squares 5″ × 5″.

RED

- Cut 1 strip 5″ × the width of fabric.
  Subcut 4 squares 5″ × 5″.
- Cut 8 strips 4½″ × the width of fabric.
  Subcut 4 rectangles 4½″ × 24½″.
  Subcut 4 rectangles 4½″ × 20½″.

ORANGE

- Cut 3 strips 5″ × the width of fabric.
  Subcut 22 squares 5″ × 5″.

WHITE

- Cut 5 strips 5″ × the width of fabric.
  Subcut 38 squares 5″ × 5″.
- Cut 8 strips 4½″ × the width of fabric.
  Subcut 4 rectangles 4½″ × 28½″.
  Subcut 4 rectangles 4½″ × 24½″.
  Subcut 4 rectangles 4½″ × 12½″.
  Subcut 4 rectangles 4½″ × 8½″.

Quilt Construction

When you make the half-square triangles, press the seams toward the darker fabric. Press all other seams according to the arrows in the diagrams.

Half-Square Triangles

Referring to Half-Square Triangles (page 60), make the number of half-square triangles in the color combinations shown in the chart. Trim each to 4½″ × 4½″.

NUMBER OF 5″ SQUARES	NUMBER OF HALF-SQUARE TRIANGLES
6 pink	12
6 white	
6 blue	12
6 white	
12 yellow	24
12 white	
14 orange	28
14 white	
4 purple	8
4 blue	
4 green	8
4 yellow	
4 green	8
4 orange	
4 red	8
4 orange	

Quilt Quarters

Lay out a quarter of the quilt as shown. Get happy that you've got all the lines flowing in the right direction.

1. Sew the units into rows.

2. Sew Row 1 to Row 2.

3. Sew Row 3 to the bottom of Row 2.

4. Sew Row 4 to the sides of Rows 1/2/3.

5. Continue to add rows in numerical order until the quilt quarter is complete.

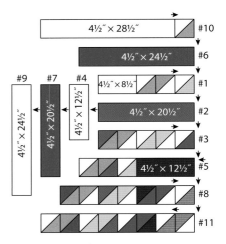

Quilt quarter. Make 4.

Quilt Assembly

Sew the 4 quarters together—the seams should nest nicely for you! Press the final seams open to reduce bulk.

Quilting and Finishing

Quilt and bind the quilt as desired. Cheryl Ferris quilted both of these quilts with an allover pantograph design called *All Leaf Simple* by Kim Diamond of Sweet Dreams Quilt Studio.

Make your own quilt coloring page! Make an enlarged copy of this outline and then color it in to create your own color plan.

Betsy's Scrappy Quilt

The scrappy version of this quilt quickly became my favorite! To make this especially scrappy, I pieced the long rectangles with several scrap-fabric squares instead of cutting them in one long piece. All the yardage requirements are the same.

Betsy's Scrappy Quilt, 64½˝ × 64½˝, made by Joyce Dean Gieszler, quilted by Cheryl Ferris, 2014

Spinning Triangles

Finished units: 9″ × 9″ • Finished quilt: 54½″ × 54½″

Spinning Triangles, 54½″ × 54½″, made by Joyce Dean Gieszler, quilted by Cheryl Ferris, 2014

Materials

The feature project uses scraps for a lively mix of colors. For a consistent colorway using yardage, see Old-Fashioned Spinning Triangles (page 17).

WHITE 2⅞ yards

ASSORTED PRINTS: 1⅝ yards

BINDING: ½ yard

BACKING: 3½ yards

BATTING: 62″ × 62″

I had lots of bright scraps left over from three different quilts and knew they needed a spectacular project. I've always loved this traditional pattern, but I wanted unbroken white space to show off fabulous quilting. I redesigned the pattern to make the cutting and sewing much easier. This was one of those times when I was really happy to have a bolt of white fabric on hand—I could just get started right away. You can't go wrong with a large piece of solid white fabric. I wanted the background to be in high contrast to the scraps to really let the pattern sing.

Cutting

WHITE

- Cut 7 strips 2½″ × the width of fabric.

  Subcut 108 squares 2½″ × 2½″ for the half-square triangles. Draw a diagonal line from one corner to the opposite corner on the back of each.

- Cut 1 strip 10¼″ × the width of fabric.

  Subcut 3 squares 10¼″ × 10¼″. Cut each twice on the diagonal to yield 12 triangles.

- Cut 2 strips 9½″ × the width of fabric.

  Subcut 4 squares 9½″ × 9½″.

  Subcut 8 rectangles 9½″ × 5″.

- Cut 3 strips 6¾″ × the width of fabric.

  Subcut 12 squares 6¾″ × 6¾″.

- Cut 4 strips 5½″ × the width of fabric.

  Subcut 22 squares 5½″ × 5½″. Cut 18 squares once on the diagonal to yield 36 triangles. Trim the remaining 4 squares to 5″ × 5″.

ASSORTED PRINTS

- Cut 108 squares 2½″ × 2½″ for the half-square triangles.

- Cut 18 squares 5½″ × 5½″. Cut each once on the diagonal to yield 36 triangles.

- Cut 54 squares 3½″ × 3½″. Cut each twice on the diagonal to yield 216 triangles.

BINDING

- Cut 6 strips 2¼″ × the width of fabric.

Quilt Construction

You may want to test your ¼˝ seam allowance before starting this quilt. When you make the half-square triangles, press the seams toward the print fabric. Press all other seams according to the arrows in the diagrams.

Half-Square Triangles

Referring to Half-Square Triangles (page 60), use the 2½˝ × 2½˝ squares in white and assorted prints to make 216 half-square triangles. Trim each to 2˝ × 2˝.

Block A

1. Arrange 3 half-square triangles and 3 triangles cut from the assorted 3½˝ × 3½˝ squares as shown. Stitch together in rows and then sew the rows together to make a Triple T unit.

Triple T unit. Make 36.

2. Line up a ruler so the ¼˝ mark just touches the intersection of the triangles on the diagonal edge of the Triple T unit. Trim the seam allowance to ¼˝.

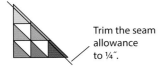

Trim the seam allowance to ¼˝.

3. Sew 1 Triple T unit to a triangle cut from the white 5½˝ × 5½˝ squares. Press the seam toward the white fabric. You may need to square up the block slightly to 5˝ × 5˝.

Make 36.

4. Sew together 4 of the units created in Step 3 into a pinwheel. Note the correct placement of the triangles.

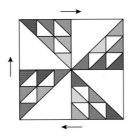

Block A. Make 9.

Block B

1. Referring to the instructions in Block A, Step 1, make another 36 Triple T units. *Do not trim!* Set aside 12 Triple T units for Block C.

2. Sew an untrimmed Triple T unit to one side of a white 6¾˝ × 6¾˝ square. Press the seam allowance toward the white. Attach another untrimmed Triple T unit to the opposite side of the square.

Note ------------------------------

Place the white square on top when sewing to minimize stretching the bias edge of the Triple T unit.
----

3. Sew a triangle cut from the print 5½˝ × 5½˝ squares to each of the remaining sides of the white square.

4. Square up the block to 9½˝ × 9½˝, if necessary.

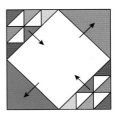

Block B. Make 12.

Block C

Block C is really a Flying Geese block with one of the half-square triangles made from smaller half-square triangles. For each block, you will need 1 large white triangle, 1 print triangle, and 1 Triple T unit, which you set aside while making Block B.

1. Sew the Triple T unit to the right side of the white triangle.

2. Sew the print triangle to the left side of the white triangle.

3. Trim the block to 5˝ × 9½˝, if necessary.

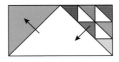

Block C. Make 12.

Quilt Assembly

1. Lay out the quilt in rows as shown in the quilt assembly diagram. Get happy that you've got all the triangles flowing in the right direction.

Note ------------------------------

A cautionary tale: I laid out all of my blocks, took a photograph, and merrily sewed them together. After getting the quilt back from the quilter, I realized I had turned two of the blocks! I spent two days taking out quilting stitches and turning those blocks. Please, please, please be careful. Make sure that the half-square triangle units look like spinning propeller blades. You'll be glad you did!

----

2. Sew the blocks together in rows, and then sew the rows together.

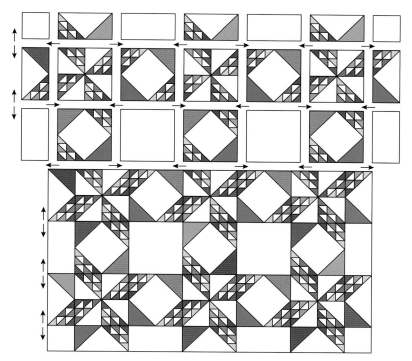

Quilt assembly

Quilting and Finishing

Quilt and bind the quilt as desired. Cheryl Ferris quilted this with an allover pantograph design called *Topiary Hearts* by Patricia E. Ritter of Urban Elementz.

Make your own quilt coloring page! Make an enlarged copy of this outline and then color it in to create your own color plan.

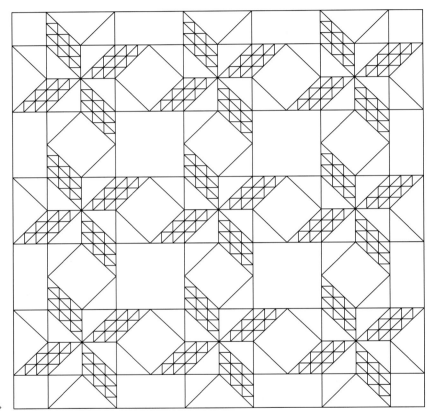

Old-Fashioned Spinning Triangles

I knew I wanted a vintage counterpart to this bright, scrappy quilt. Friends clamored for me to use more purple, and I listened in a big way. AnnMarie Cowley quilted this with straight lines spaced ¼″ apart. The modern quilting is a perfect complement to the old-fashioned pattern. All the yardage requirements are the same.

Old-Fashioned Spinning Triangles, 54½″ × 54½″, made by Joyce Dean Gieszler, quilted by AnnMarie Cowley, 2015

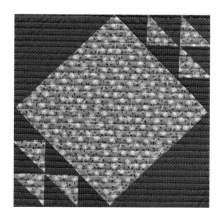

Chain and Bar

Finished block: 16″ × 16″ • Finished quilt: 64½″ × 64½″

Chain and Bar, 64½″ × 64½″, made by Joyce Dean Gieszler, quilted by Cheryl Ferris, 2015

Materials

The feature project uses scraps for a lively mix of colors. For a consistent colorway using yardage, see Holiday Chain and Bar *(page 25).*

CREAM 2 yards

PINK 1⅛ yards

RED 1¾ yards (includes binding)

BLUE 1⅓ yards

BLACK 1⅛ yards

BACKING: 4 yards

BATTING: 72″ × 72″

I fell in love with this quilt block because it is so versatile. I had a lot of fun with a coloring page working out all the possibilities. The pink/red/blue/black version was inspired by a presentation on Pendleton Woolen Mills and their lovely products. My mother worked at one of their factories when I was a young child, and I have always appreciated their saturated colors and quality products.

I had the red fabric left over from another quilt, and I let it guide my selection of fabric colors. A few years ago, I decided that I needed more neutral fabrics in my stash, and I made a point of buying neutrals in two-yard cuts. I've never been sorry I did that, because they have worked their way into a lot of projects.

I created the green-and-red version by coloring a line drawing of the quilt blocks. I love the diagonal look and cheery holiday colors.

Cutting

Note

This pattern calls for you to make flying geese units using the four-at-a-time method. The cutting instructions show cutting small 2⅞″ × 2⅞″ squares and large 5¼″ × 5¼″ squares. This will produce a unit exactly 2½″ × 4½″. I prefer to make my pieces oversized and trim them to the correct size after piecing, so I started with small 3¼″ × 3¼″ squares and large 5¾″ × 5¾″ squares, and then I trimmed the unit to the exact size. Both methods work just fine—you just need to decide which method to stick with before you start cutting! Enough yardage is built into the fabric requirements to allow for oversized cutting. For the quarter-square triangles, I've given you cutting instructions for over-sized 5½″ × 5½″ squares so you can trim down your units.

CREAM

- Cut 4 strips 7″ × the width of fabric.

  Subcut 20 squares 7″ × 7″ for the large half-square triangles.

- Cut 2 strips 5½″ × the width of fabric.

  Subcut 8 squares 5½″ × 5½″ for the quarter-square triangles.

- Cut 8 strips 2⅞″ × the width of fabric.*

  Subcut 96 squares 2⅞″ × 2⅞″ for the flying geese units.

PINK

- Cut 2 strips 7″ × the width of fabric.

  Subcut 10 squares 7″ × 7″ for the large half-square triangles.

- Cut 1 strip 6½″ × the width of fabric.

  Subcut 8 rectangles 6½″ × 4½″ for the bars.

- Cut 1 strip 5½″ × the width of fabric.

  Subcut 2 squares 5½″ × 5½″ for the quarter-square triangles.

- Cut 1 strip 5¼″ × the width of fabric.*

  Subcut 6 squares 5¼″ × 5¼″ for the flying geese units.

RED

- Cut 3 strips 7″ × the width of fabric.

  Subcut 12 squares 7″ × 7″ for the large half-square triangles.

- Cut 1 strip 6½″ × the width of fabric.

  Subcut 8 rectangles 6½″ × 4½″ for the bars.

- Cut 1 strip 5½″ × the width of fabric.

  Subcut 2 squares 5½″ × 5½″ for the quarter-square triangles.

- Cut 1 strip 5¼″ × the width of fabric.*

  Subcut 6 squares 5¼″ × 5¼″ for the flying geese units.

- Cut 7 strips 2¼″ × the width of fabric for the binding.

BLUE

- Cut 3 strips 7″ × the width of fabric.

  Subcut 12 squares 7″ × 7″ for the large half-square triangles.

- Cut 1 strip 6½″ × the width of fabric.

  Subcut 8 rectangles 6½″ × 4½″ for the bars.

- Cut 1 strip 5½″ × the width of fabric.

  Subcut 2 squares 5½″ × 5½″ for the quarter-square triangles.

- Cut 1 strip 5¼″ × the width of fabric.*

  Subcut 6 squares 5¼″ × 5¼″ for the flying geese units.

BLACK

- Cut 2 strips 7″ × the width of fabric.

  Subcut 10 squares 7″ × 7″ for the large half-square triangles.

- Cut 1 strip 6½″ × the width of fabric.

  Subcut 8 rectangles 6½″ × 4½″ for the bars.

- Cut 1 strip 5½″ × the width of fabric.

  Subcut 2 squares 5½″ × 5½″ for the quarter-square triangles.

- Cut 1 strip 5¼″ × the width of fabric.*

  Subcut 6 squares 5¼″ × 5¼″ for the flying geese units.

See the cutting note (previous page) before cutting flying geese units.

Quilt Construction

When you make the half-square triangles, press the seams toward the darker fabric.
Press all other seams according to the arrows in the diagrams.

Half-Square Triangles

Referring to Half-Square Triangles (page 60), make the number of half-square triangles shown in the chart. Trim the large half-square triangles to 6½″ × 6½″. Do not trim the small half-square triangles.

NUMBER OF SQUARES	SIZE OF SQUARES	NUMBER OF HALF-SQUARE TRIANGLES
6 pink 6 cream	7″ × 7″	12
4 pink 4 red	7″ × 7″	8
4 red 4 cream	7″ × 7″	8
4 red 4 blue	7″ × 7″	8
4 blue 4 cream	7″ × 7″	8
4 blue 4 black	7″ × 7″	8
6 black 6 cream	7″ × 7″	12
2 pink 2 cream	5½″ × 5½″	4
2 red 2 cream	5½″ × 5½″	4
2 blue 2 cream	5½″ × 5½″	4
2 black 2 cream	5½″ × 5½″	4

Quarter-Square Triangles

Referring to Quarter-Square Triangles (page 60), pair the small half-square triangles made as shown in the chart to make finished quarter-square triangles. Square up each to 4½″ × 4½″.

NUMBER OF HALF-SQUARE TRIANGLES	NUMBER OF QUARTER-SQUARE TRIANGLES
4 pink/cream	4
4 red/cream	4
4 blue/cream	4
4 black/cream	4

Chain Sewing ---------------------------------------

Chain sewing, or speed piecing, is when you sew one unit right after the other without cutting the threads. After the first unit is sewn, take a couple of stitches off the edge of the piece, raise your presser foot (if necessary), and insert the second unit. Sew across that unit, take a couple of stitches off the edge, and so forth. Continue in this manner until all units are sewn. Remove the "chain" from the machine, clip the units apart, and press. Chain sewing saves time and thread.

An advantage to chain sewing is that you can stack up a large number of units and just keep sewing. You don't have to stop to press each time. A disadvantage is that you can sit at your sewing machine for a *very* long time, and that's not good for your body. Another disadvantage is that if you make an error, you've repeated it several times! After sewing a few units, I always stop to check that I'm putting the units together correctly.

Flying Geese

1. On the back of each cream square, draw a diagonal pencil line from one corner to the opposite corner.

2. Place 2 cream 2⅞″ × 2⅞″ squares on opposite corners of a pink 5¼″ × 5¼″ square, with the pencil lines aligned.

3. Sew ¼″ from each side of the drawn centerline.

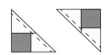

4. Cut apart on the diagonal line.

5. Press the seams toward the cream fabric.

6. With right sides together, place a cream 2⅞″ × 2⅞″ square on the corner of each unit, with the drawn centerline perpendicular to the original seam.

7. Sew ¼″ from each side of the drawn centerline.

8. Cut apart on the diagonal line.

9. Press the seams toward the cream fabric.

Make 24.

10. Repeat Steps 2–9 for red, blue, and black Flying Geese.

Make 24.

Make 24.

Make 24.

Flying Flock

Use the flying geese units you just made to assemble these flocks of geese.

Make 8.

Make 8.

Make 8.

Make 8.

Assembling the Blocks

1. Lay out the half-square triangles, bars, flying flocks, and quarter-square triangle units as shown.

2. Sew into rows and then sew the rows together.

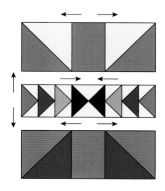

Make 2.

Make 2.

Make 2.

Make 2.

Make 2.

Make 2.

Make 2.

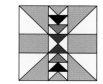

Make 2.

Quilt Assembly

1. Arrange the quilt blocks as shown in the quilt assembly diagram. Pay particular attention to the orientation of the blocks to maintain the sense of one color spilling into another.

2. Sew the blocks together in rows, and then sew the rows together.

Quilt assembly

Quilting and Finishing

Quilt and bind as desired. Cheryl Ferris quilted this scrappy top with an allover pantograph design called *Fork in the Road* by Barbara Becker of Urban Elementz.

Make your own quilt coloring page! Make an enlarged copy of this outline and then color it in to create your own color plan.

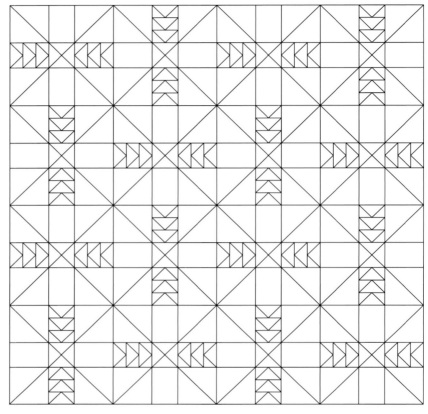

Holiday Chain and Bar

Brighten up your holidays with this diagonal quilt. It would also look great in school colors for your favorite graduate! To make this quilt, use 2¾ yards of cream fabric, 1¾ yards of red fabric, and 2¾ yards of green fabric. Green is one of those fabrics I collect when I find it because the shades change so often—olive green, poison green, yellow green, muted green, and so on. When I find the perfect color, I buy three yards. Again, lucky me that I had this green on hand.

Cheryl Ferris quilted this top with an allover pantograph design called *All Leaf Simple* by Kim Diamond of Sweet Dreams Quilt Studio.

Holiday Chain and Bar, 64½″ × 64½″, made by Joyce Dean Gieszler, quilted by Cheryl Ferris, 2015

Make the following units:

- Half-square triangles: 32 green, 32 red
- Quarter-square triangles: 16 green/red/cream
- Flying Geese: 48 green, 48 red
- Bars: 13 green, 13 red, 6 cream

Make 6 (Blocks 1, 6, 8, 9, 11, 16).

Make 3 (Blocks 4, 12, 14).

Make 1 (Block 3).

Make 4 (Blocks 2, 7, 10, 15).

Make 2 (Blocks 5, 13).

1	2	3	4
5	6	7	8
9	10	11	12
13	14	15	16

Block placement

Confetti

Finished block: 17½″ × 17½″ • Finished quilt: 78″ × 78″

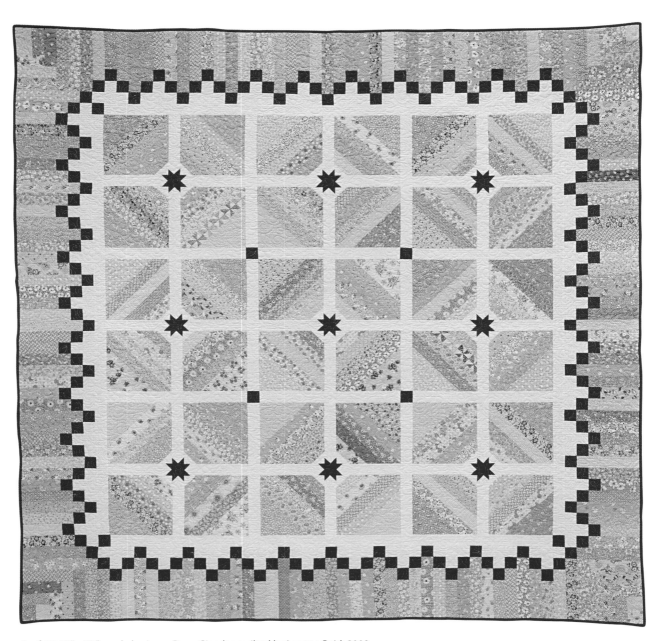

Confetti, 78″ × 78″, made by Joyce Dean Gieszler, quilted by Leanne Reid, 2009

Materials

The feature project uses scraps for a lively mix of colors. For a consistent colorway using yardage, see Confetti Blues (page 33).

I like balanced colors in my designs. Look closely and you'll see that there are no red scraps in this quilt. That was intentional, because I was using red as my pop of color. I used equal amounts of green, blue, yellow, purple, pink, and orange throughout the quilt. As you can see by the cutting instructions, this is a great quilt to use up those 2˝ strips of fabric!

1930s SCRAPS: 6 yards for the blocks and border (largest pieces are 8˝ square and 2˝ × 14˝)

RED 1⅓ yards for the cornerstones, border, and binding

WHITE 2¼ yards

BACKING: 7¼ yards

BATTING: 86˝ × 86˝

RULER: 8½˝ × 8½˝ ruler or 9 pieces of freezer paper cut to 8½˝ × 8½˝

Years ago, I moved my sewing room and found I had an abundance of 1930s scraps. When I started sorting them, it looked like confetti on my cutting table! So I designed this quilt to be bright and fun—a festive event. It makes me smile every time I look at it.

I've seen this quilt made in 28 shades of gray; red, white, and blue; taupe, muslin, and brown; and orange, purple, and pink batiks. They were all fabulous.

Cutting

SCRAPS FOR BLOCKS

- Cut 18 squares 8˝ × 8˝.

  Subcut each square once on the diagonal to yield 36 large triangles.

- Cut 72 rectangles 2˝ × 14˝.
- Cut 36 rectangles 2˝ × 11˝.
- Cut 36 rectangles 2˝ × 8˝.

SCRAPS FOR BORDER

- Cut 8 rectangles 2¼˝ × 2½˝.
- Cut 8 rectangles 2˝ × 4˝.
- Cut 48 rectangles 2˝ × 5½˝.
- Cut 88 rectangles 2˝ × 7˝.
- Cut 48 rectangles 2˝ × 8½˝.

RED

- Cut 9 strips 2˝ × the width of fabric. Set aside 6 strips for the border.

  From the remaining 3 strips, subcut 57 squares 2˝ × 2˝.

- Cut 3 strips 1¼˝ × the width of fabric.

  Subcut 72 squares 1¼˝ × 1¼˝.

- Cut 9 strips 2¼˝ × the width of fabric for the binding.

WHITE

- Cut 25 strips 2˝ × the width of fabric. Set aside 10 strips for the borders.

  From 6 strips, subcut 12 rectangles 2˝ × 18˝ for the large block sashing.

  From 9 strips, subcut 36 rectangles 2˝ × 8½˝ for the star sashing.

- Cut 2 strips 3½˝ × the width of fabric for the border.

- Cut 2 strips 4˝ × the width of fabric.

  Subcut 18 squares 4˝ × 4˝. Cut each square once on the diagonal to yield 36 small triangles.

Quilt Construction

Press all seams according to the arrows in the diagrams.

Small Blocks

Be sure each block contains a variety of prints and colors. This block is sewn oversized and trimmed later, so you don't have to spend a lot of time centering the pieces exactly. Close is good enough! Handle the triangles gently, though, because they are cut on the bias.

For each small block, you need:

- 1 small white triangle
- 1 rectangle 2″ × 8″
- 1 rectangle 2″ × 11″
- 2 rectangles 2″ × 14″
- 1 large scrap triangle

1. Mark the centers of the long sides of a small white triangle and a 2″ × 8″ scrap rectangle. I usually just finger-press the pieces in half to find the centers.

2. Right sides together and centers aligned, stitch the triangle and rectangle together along their longest sides.

3. Add the next 3 pieces in the same manner—first the 2″ × 11″ rectangle, then the 2 rectangles 2″ × 14″, followed by the large scrap triangle.

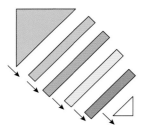

Small block. Make 36.

4. To square up the block, center an 8½″ ruler with the diagonal line (shown in the diagram below as a solid line) placed between the 2″ × 14″ rectangles. Trim the blocks to 8½″ × 8½″. If you use freezer paper, iron an 8½″ × 8½″ square to the block, lining it up as shown in the diagram. Trim, using a ruler and rotary cutter.

Note --

If you don't have an 8½″ ruler, a freezer paper template with a diagonal line drawn on it is a quick and easy way to "mark" the square for trimming. Press the freezer paper to the block with a dry iron and trim using a ruler and rotary cutter. You can reuse your freezer-paper template; they generally have a lifespan of four uses.

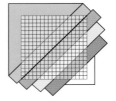

Star Sashing

1. Draw a diagonal line from one corner to the opposite corner on the wrong side of all red 1¼″ × 1¼″ squares. Right sides together, place a red square on the corner of a white 2″ × 8½″ sashing piece. Stitch on the drawn line.

2. Trim the seam to ¼″. Press the triangle toward the corner of the block.

3. Repeat with another red square on the adjoining corner.

Star sashing. Make 36.

Note ---

At this point, I like to arrange all 36 small blocks so I can see the overall effect and balance the colors. Once I'm happy, I sew the blocks together in sets of 4 to make large blocks.

Large Blocks

Arrange 4 small blocks, 1 red 2″ × 2″ square, and 4 star sashing units as shown. Sew together.

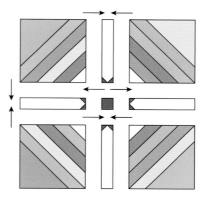

Large block. Make 9.

Quilt Center

1. Assemble the quilt center by arranging the blocks in a 3 × 3 formation, with sashing and cornerstones in between, as shown in the quilt assembly diagram (page 31).

2. Sew the blocks into rows and then sew the rows together.

Inner Border

1. Sew 6 white 2″ strips together and trim 4 border rectangles to measure 2″ × 56″. If your quilt has a different measurement, make the inner border to that measurement.

2. Attach the side borders and press the seams toward the border.

3. Sew a 2″ × 2″ red square to each end of the top and bottom borders. Press the seams toward the borders.

4. Stitch the top and bottom borders to the quilt. Press the seams toward the borders.

Outer Border

1. Stitch a 2″ white strip and a 2″ red strip together to make a strip set. Make 4. Subcut 80 units 2″ × 3½″.

Subcut 80 units.

2. Stitch a 3½″ white strip and a 2″ red strip together to make a strip set. Make 2. Subcut 40 units 2″ × 5″.

Subcut 40 units.

3. Sew a 3½″ red/white unit to a 2″ × 7″ scrap rectangle. Make 80.

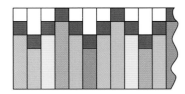

Make 80.

4. Sew a 5″ red/white unit to a 2″ × 5½″ scrap rectangle. Make 40.

Make 40.

5. Sew a 2″ × 2″ red square to a 2″ × 8½″ scrap rectangle. Make 36.

Make 36.

6. Arrange the border pieces as shown. The sequence for the scrap pieces is 7″, 5½″, 7″, 8½″, 7″, 5½″, 7″, 8½″, and so on. Beginning with a 7″ scrap unit, sew 39 units together to complete 1 border. Make 4.

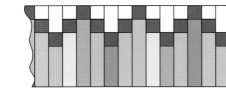

Make 4.

Corner Blocks

1. Lay out the following scrap pieces for each corner block:

- 2 rectangles 2¼˝ × 2½˝
- 2 rectangles 2˝ × 4˝
- 2 rectangles 2˝ × 5½˝
- 2 rectangles 2˝ × 7˝
- 3 rectangles 2˝ × 8½˝

2. Sew the 2¼˝ × 2½˝ rectangles together along the 2½˝ sides. Continue to add rectangles along the side and bottom of the block in numerical order, as shown, stopping at strip 9. Press the seams as indicated by the arrows in the diagram.

3. For the last side of the block, sew a red 2˝ × 2˝ square to a scrap 2˝ × 8½˝ rectangle. Add the unit to the block, placing the red square in the corner opposite the beginning square.

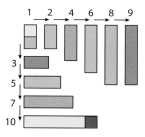

Make 4.

Quilt Assembly

Refer to the quilt assembly diagram.

1. Stitch the side borders in place. Press the seams toward the inner border.

2. Sew a corner block to each end of the top and bottom borders. Press the seams toward the corner block.

3. Stitch the top and bottom borders to the quilt. Press the seams toward the inner border.

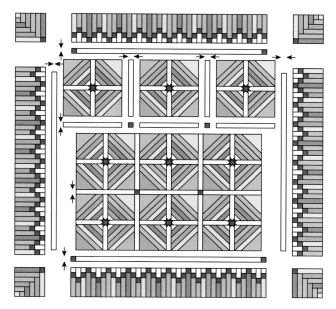

Quilt assembly

Quilting and Finishing

Quilt and bind the quilt as desired. Leanne Reid custom quilted this scrappy top with a dainty floral pattern. *Lulu Flower*, an allover pantograph design by Peg Lindberg of Apricot Moon Designs, would look adorable as well.

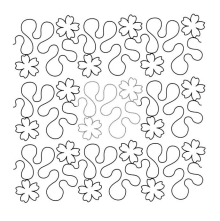

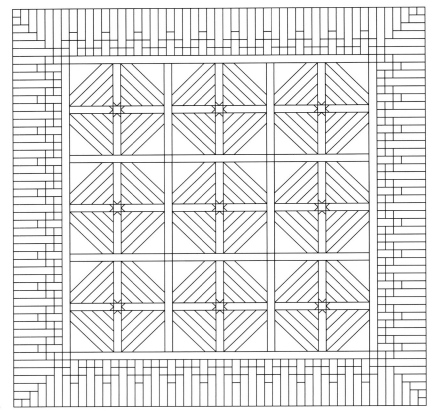

Make your own quilt coloring page! Make an enlarged copy of this outline and then color it in to create your own color plan.

Confetti Blues, 78″ × 78″, made by Joyce Dean Gieszler, quilted by Cheryl Ferris, 2015

Confetti Blues

The blue version of this quilt reminds me a bit of a swimming pool and a bit of fine china. Maybe I need a cup of tea beside a pool! I used 6 cuts, 1 yard each, in place of the scraps for this quilt. All other yardages remain the same. I used 1 blue fabric in place of the red in *Confetti*. I used the other 5 fabrics in equal amounts; where the pattern calls for 48 rectangles, I cut 10 of each to yield 50. Having extra rectangles gave me more flexibility when laying out the blocks and borders. Cheryl Ferris quilted the blue version of this top with an allover pantograph design that is no longer available. *Dogwood Pano 2* by Kim Diamond of Sweet Dreams Quilt Studio would look fabulous.

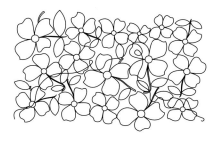

What's Up

Finished block: 9″ × 9″ • Finished quilt: 51½″ × 51½″

What's Up, 51½″ × 51½″, made by Joyce Dean Gieszler, quilted by AnnMarie Cowley, 2012

Materials

The feature project uses scraps for a lively mix of colors. For a consistent colorway using yardage, see What's Up Black and White *(page 39).*

WHITE 2¼ yards

BLACK ⅝ yard

BLUE 1 yard

RED 1 yard

GREEN ½ yard

BINDING: ½ yard

BACKING: 3½ yards

BATTING: 60″ × 60″

This quilt is very simple to make yet produces striking results. It is made from only three different units—short rails, long rails, and quarter-square triangles.

I designed the colors in reverse on this quilt, choosing the striped binding fabric first. The colors in the binding led me to the color combination shown here. I confess I bought every piece of fabric for this quilt at one store! Mind you, this store has more than 40,000 square feet of retail space and offers home dec, clothing, and wedding fabrics. It's easy to get overwhelmed when there's a sale and I have an itch to sew a new project. I had all sorts of fabrics in my cart, but when I found the binding stripe, I put everything back and began again, focusing on the colors shown here. I wasn't sure what I was going to do with the fabrics, so I bought a yard of each. They turned out to be perfect for *What's Up*. I used some of the leftover scraps in *Spinning Triangles* (page 12).

My next one is going to be in Halloween colors! Yes, I have already bought the binding fabric. On a side note, if I find a great striped fabric, I buy a yard to have on hand for binding even the largest quilt.

The alternate colorway is a simple two-color quilt in Civil War–era reproduction fabrics that looks like a bit of an optical illusion.

Cutting

WHITE

- Cut 7 strips 4½″ × the width of fabric.

  Subcut 54 squares 4½″ × 4½″.

- Cut 27 strips 1½″ × the width of fabric.

  Subcut each strip in half to yield 54 strips 1½″ × approximately 20″.

BLACK

- Cut 2 strips 4½″ × the width of fabric.

  Subcut 9 squares 4½″ × 4½″.

- Cut 5 strips 1½″ × the width of fabric.

  Subcut each strip in half to yield 10 strips 1½″ × approximately 20″.

BLUE

- Cut 3 strips 4½″ × the width of fabric.

  Subcut 20 squares 4½″ × 4½″.

- Cut 11 strips 1½″ × the width of fabric.

  Subcut each strip in half to yield 22 strips 1½″ × approximately 20″.

RED

- Cut 3 strips 4½″ × the width of fabric.

  Subcut 18 squares 4½″ × 4½″.

- Cut 9 strips 1½″ × the width of fabric.

  Subcut each strip in half to yield 18 strips 1½″ × approximately 20″.

GREEN

- Cut 1 strip 4½″ × the width of fabric.

  Subcut 7 squares 4½″ × 4½″.

- Cut 3 strips 1½″ × the width of fabric.

  Subcut each strip in half to yield 6 strips 1½″ × approximately 20″.

BINDING STRIPE

- Cut 6 strips 2¼″ × the width of fabric.

Quilt Construction

You may want to test your ¼″ seam allowance before starting this quilt. When you make the half-square triangles, press the seams toward the darker fabric. Press all other seams according to the arrows in the diagrams.

Rail Units

Make 3-part strip sets by sewing the 1½″ strips together along the 20″ sides. Press the seams toward the darker fabric. Your strip sets should measure 3½″ × approximately 20″. Refer to the chart to make the correct number of strip sets from each color combination and to see how many rails to subcut.

Sample strip set using 1½″ strips

Subcut 9½″ and 3½″ rails from each strip set. I recommend cutting all the 9½″ rails first, then the 3½″ rails.

STRIP-SET FABRICS	NUMBER OF 20″ STRIP SETS	NUMBER OF 9½″ RAILS	NUMBER OF 3½″ RAILS
White-black-white	3	4	4
Black-white-black	3	4	4
Blue-white-blue	7	8	12
White-blue-white	7	8	12
Red-white-red	6	6	12
White-red-white	6	6	12
Green-white-green	2	2	4
White-green-white	2	2	4

Quarter-Square Triangles

1. Referring to Half-Square Triangles (page 60), make the number of half-square triangles in the color combinations shown in the chart. Do not trim!

NUMBER OF 4½˝ SQUARES	NUMBER OF HALF-SQUARE TRIANGLES
9 white 9 black	18
20 white 20 blue	40
18 white 18 red	36
7 white 7 green	14

2. Referring to Quarter-Square Triangles (page 60), pair the half-square triangles listed in the chart to make the finished quarter-square triangles. Square each quarter-square triangle to 3½˝ × 3½˝.

NUMBER OF HALF-SQUARE TRIANGLES	NUMBER OF QUARTER-SQUARE TRIANGLES
8 black/white	8
10 black/white 10 blue/white	20
14 blue/white	14
15 blue/white 15 red/white	30
14 red/white	14
7 red/white 7 green/white	14
6 green/white	6

Block Construction

For this quilt, you will make 1 block in 3 color variations.

1. Lay out the rail units and quarter-square triangles as shown.

2. Sew into rows, and then sew the rows together.

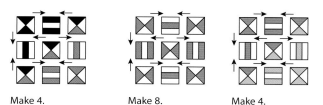

Make 4. Make 8. Make 4.

Sashing

Stitch the sashing units together.

Make 2.

Make 1.

Quilt Quarters

This quilt is made in 4 quarters. Lay out the blocks and units as shown. Pay close attention to the orientation of the blocks so the diagonal pattern flows! Sew the rows together, pressing the seams open to reduce bulk.

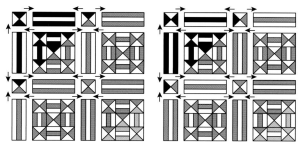

Make 2. Make 2.

Quilt Assembly

1. Refer to the quilt assembly diagram to arrange the quarters.

2. Sew the quarters together.

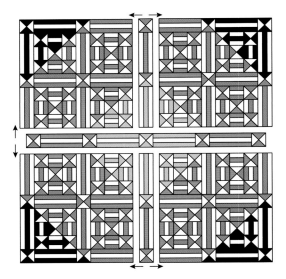

Quilt assembly

Quilting and Finishing

Quilt and bind your quilt as desired. AnnMarie Cowley custom quilted this scrappy top. She stitched straight lines to emphasize the arrows of the pattern.

Make your own quilt coloring page! Make an enlarged copy of this outline and then color it in to create your own color plan.

What's Up Black and White, 51½″ × 51½″, made by Joyce Dean Gieszler, quilted by Cheryl Ferris, 2015

What's Up Black and White

The scrappy version of this quilt was so "diagonal" that I wanted to see what would happen if I just made sixteen identical blocks. I love the graphic element of this quilt! Black fabric is another colorway that I like to collect when I find a great print with a small pattern. In this case, however, I went looking for a specific black that looked great with the white shirting print I had on hand.

To make the quilt, use 2¼ yards of white fabric for the blocks and sashing, and use 2¾ yards of black fabric for the blocks, sashing, and binding. Make sixteen identical blocks.

Cheryl Ferris quilted the black-and-white version with an allover pantograph design called *All Leaf Simple* by Kim Diamond of Sweet Dreams Quilt Studio.

Snowbirds

Finished block: 12″ × 12″ • Finished quilt: 60½″ × 72½″

Snowbirds, 60½″ × 72½″, made by Joyce Dean Gieszler, quilted by Cheryl Ferris, 2015

Materials

The feature project uses scraps, but in a limited color range. For an even more consistent colorway using yardage, see College Bound (page 45).

ASSORTED BLUE PRINTS: 2 yards for the blocks and half of the binding

WHITE SNOWFLAKE: 1½ yards for use with blue fabrics

ASSORTED AQUA PRINTS: 1¾ yards for the blocks and half of the binding

WHITE POLKA DOT: 1½ yards for use with aqua fabrics

ASSORTED RED PRINTS: ¼ yard

BACKING: 4 yards

BATTING: 69″ × 81″

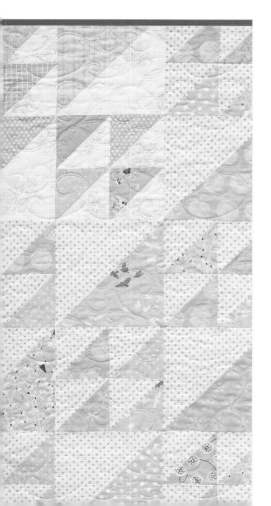

This quilt is made from the traditional Flock of Geese block and reminds me of family members who go south every year and those who live far away. My husband and I have 2 children, and they live 2,000 miles apart from one another. While we travel to see them, our hearts are always somewhere in the middle.

Cutting

ASSORTED BLUE PRINTS

- Cut 15 squares 7″ × 7″.
- Cut 57 squares 4″ × 4″.
- Cut 4 strips 2¼″ × the width of fabric for half of the binding.

WHITE SNOWFLAKE

- Cut 15 squares 7″ × 7″.
- Cut 57 squares 4″ × 4″.

ASSORTED AQUA PRINTS

- Cut 15 squares 7″ × 7″.
- Cut 59 squares 4″ × 4″.
- Cut 4 strips 2¼″ × the width of fabric for half of the binding.

WHITE POLKA DOT

- Cut 15 squares 7″ × 7″.
- Cut 59 squares 4″ × 4″.

ASSORTED RED PRINTS

- Cut 9 squares 4″ × 4″.
- Cut 2 squares 3½″ × 3½″.

Quilt Construction

You may want to test your ¼″ seam allowance before starting this quilt. When making the half-square triangles, press the seams toward the darker fabric. Press all other seams according to the arrows in the diagrams.

Flock of Geese Blocks

1. Referring to Half-Square Triangles (page 60), make the number of half-square triangles in the colors shown in the chart. Trim the large half-square triangles to 6½″ × 6½″ and the small ones to 3½″ × 3½″.

NUMBER OF SQUARES	SIZE OF SQUARES	NUMBER OF HALF-SQUARE TRIANGLES
15 blue 15 white snowflake	7″ × 7″	30 (You will have 1 extra.)
15 aqua 15 white polka dot	7″ × 7″	30
57 blue 57 white snowflake	4″ × 4″	114
59 aqua 59 white polka dot	4″ × 4″	118
1 blue 1 red	4″ × 4″	2 (You will have 1 extra.)
1 white snowflake 1 red	4″ × 4″	2
2 white polka dot 2 red	4″ × 4″	4 (You will have 1 extra.)
6 red	4″ × 4″	6

Note ----------------------------------

You could make part of the heart from squares instead of half-square triangles, but I wanted it to be scrappy and to mimic the same design elements throughout. If you'd like to use squares, cut 6 squares 3½″ × 3½″.

----

2. Using 2 large half-square triangles and 8 small half-square triangles for each block, lay out and sew each block as shown.

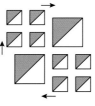

Make 14.   Make 14.

Heart Blocks

Important: See the illustration for the orientation of each block before sewing on the red square!

1. Lightly draw a diagonal line from one corner to the opposite corner on 2 red 3½˝ squares. Right sides together, place a red square on one corner of a large blue/white half-square triangle, with the line perpendicular to the centerline of the half-square triangle.

Sew directly on the line, trim the seam allowance to ¼˝, and press the seam allowance toward the red triangle.

Make 1.

2. Repeat Step 1 with a large aqua/white half-square triangle.

Make 1.

3. Lay out the half-square triangles as shown to make the 2 blocks that make up the heart in the center of the quilt. Press all seams open.

Make 1.   Make 1.

Quilt Assembly

1. Refer to the quilt assembly diagram to lay out the quilt.

2. Sew the blocks together in rows, and then sew the rows together.

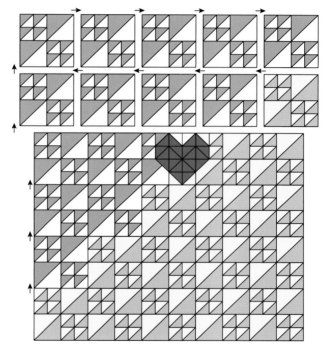

Quilt assembly

Quilting and Finishing

Quilt and bind your quilt as desired. For instructions on using two colors of binding, as I have done, see Specialty Binding (page 61). Cheryl Ferris quilted both *Snowbirds* and *College Bound* with an allover pantograph design called *Janet's Swirl* by Kim Diamond of Sweet Dreams Quilt Studio.

Make your own quilt coloring page! Make an enlarged copy of this outline and then color it in to create your own color plan.

College Bound

The alternate colorway of this quilt was designed with the University of Oregon colors (go Ducks!), and school colors are perfect for your college-bound student. Or celebrate the colors of a favorite sports team (go Green Bay!). The yardages in the alternate colorway don't change much—just replace the feature project's aqua fabric with one yellow and the blue fabric with one green, and use 2¾ yards of white for the background.

College Bound, 60½" × 72½", made by Joyce Dean Gieszler, quilted by Cheryl Ferris, 2015

Safe Travels

Finished block: 12″ × 12″ • Finished quilt: 58½″ × 58½″

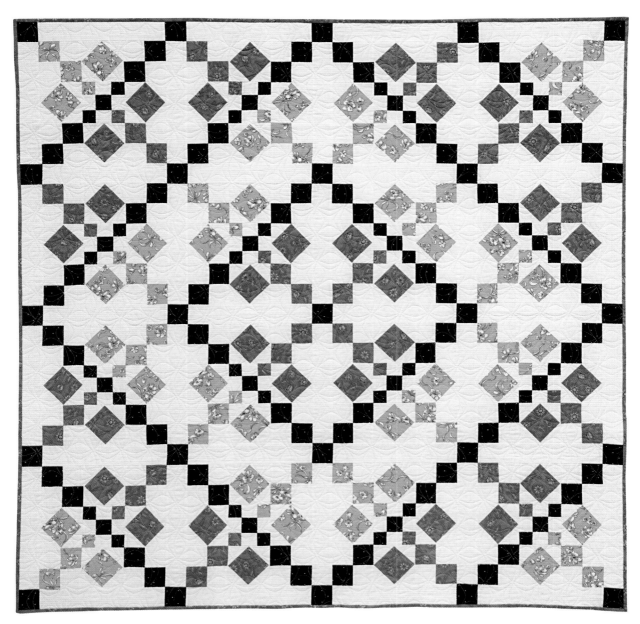

Safe Travels, 58½″ × 58½″, made by Joyce Dean Gieszler, quilted by Cheryl Ferris, 2014

Materials

The feature project uses yardage for a consistent colorway. For a scrappy version, see Flower Garden *(page 51).*

WHITE 3¼ yards

BLACK ⅝ yard

GRAY 1⅛ yards

YELLOW ⅝ yard

BACKING: 3¾ yards

BATTING: 66″ × 66″

The design created by the gray squares reminds me of airplanes crisscrossing the country and the tidy parcels of land as seen from above (think Wright Brothers!). That same gray shape reminds me of dragonflies, and I can easily picture this quilt made in greens, blues, and purples.

Cutting

WHITE

- Cut 3 strips 12½″ × the width of fabric.

    Subcut 40 rectangles 12½″ × 2½″.

- Cut 11 strips 3¼″ × the width of fabric.

    Subcut 128 squares 3¼″ × 3¼″. Cut each once on the diagonal to yield 256 triangles.

- Cut 8 strips 2½″ × the width of fabric.

- Cut 2 strips 2″ × the width of fabric.

- Cut 2 strips 1¾″ × the width of fabric.

BLACK

- Cut 4 strips 2½″ × the width of fabric.

- Cut 1 strip 2″ × the width of fabric.

- Cut 2 strips 1¾″ × the width of fabric.

GRAY

- Cut 3 strips 3¼″ × the width of fabric.

    Subcut 32 squares 3¼″ × 3¼″.

- Cut 2 strips 2½″ × the width of fabric.

- Cut 1 strip 1¾″ × the width of fabric.

- Cut 7 strips 2¼″ × the width of fabric for the binding.

YELLOW

- Cut 3 strips 3¼″ × the width of fabric.

    Subcut 32 squares 3¼″ × 3¼″.

- Cut 2 strips 2½″ × the width of fabric.

- Cut 1 strip 1¾″ × the width of fabric.

Quilt Construction

You may want to test your ¼″ seam allowance before starting this quilt.

Square-in-a-Square Units

1. Mark the center of each side of a gray 3¼″ × 3¼″ square with a small crease or pin. Matching the centers, sew a white triangle to 2 opposite sides. Trim off the dog-ears.

2. Repeat with 2 more white triangles. Trim the unit to 4½″. I intentionally made this block just a little bigger than necessary so you can trim it to the correct size.

Make 32.   Make 32.

Four-Patch Units

1. Make 2-part strip sets from the 2½″ strips. Each strip set should measure 4½″ × the width of fabric. Refer to the chart below to make the correct number of strip sets and subcut the correct number of 2½″ units.

NUMBER OF STRIPS	NUMBER OF STRIP SETS	NUMBER OF 2½″ × 4½″ UNITS
2 yellow		
2 white	2	32
2 gray		
2 white	2	32
4 black		
4 white	4	64

2. Sew the 2½″ units together in four-patches in the colorways shown.

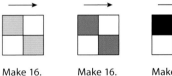

Make 16.   Make 16.   Make 32.

Uneven Nine-Patch Units

Note ---

Be careful when you're cutting and sewing these nine-patch units, because the strips and units are two different sizes!

----

1. Stitch 1¾″ strips on either side of a 2″ strip along the long sides to make 1 strip set in each of the 3 colorways. Press the seams toward the darker fabrics. The strip sets should measure 4½″ wide. Refer to the chart to make the strip sets in the correct color combinations and to subcut the correct number of units.

COLORS AND SIZES OF STRIPS	NUMBER OF UNITS
1¾″ yellow	
2″ white	16 units 1¾″ wide
1¾″ black	
1¾ white	
2″ black	16 units 2″ wide
1¾″ white	
1¾″ black	
2″ white	16 units 1¾″ wide
1¾″ gray	

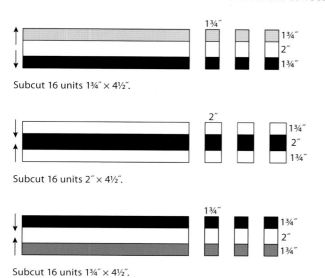

Subcut 16 units 1¾″ × 4½″.

Subcut 16 units 2″ × 4½″.

Subcut 16 units 1¾″ × 4½″.

2. Sew the 1¾″ and 2″ units together as shown. Press the seams open.

Make 16.

Block Construction

1. Lay out the four-patches, square-in-a-square units, and nine-patches.

2. Sew them into rows and sew the rows together.

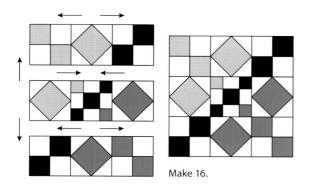

Make 16.

Quilt Assembly

1. Refer to the quilt assembly diagram to lay out the blocks, sashings, and cornerstones.

2. Sew the blocks together in rows, and then sew the rows together.

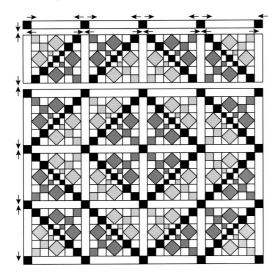

Quilt assembly

Quilting and Finishing

Quilt and bind your quilt as desired. Cheryl Ferris quilted this top with an allover pantograph design called *Bread Basket* by Peg Lindberg of Apricot Moon Designs.

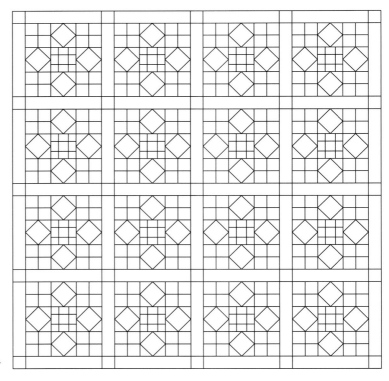

Make your own quilt coloring page! Make an enlarged copy of this outline and then color it in to create your own color plan.

Flower Garden, 58½″ × 58½″, made by Joyce Dean Gieszler, quilted by Cheryl Ferris, 2015

Flower Garden

This is another quilt that I redesigned after using a line drawing of the quilt as a coloring page. I had planned to make it in just red and white. But that color combination seemed a little dull, so I printed out the line drawing and started coloring. I get great inspiration from a box of colored pencils! I knew I wanted something scrappy to use up small bits of fabric, so I concentrated on looking at each block individually. That's when the flower garden idea was born! I worked with the color combinations to make each block look like a flower.

Cheryl Ferris quilted Flower Garden with an allover pantograph design called *Hannah's Flower* by Kim Diamond of Sweet Dreams Quilt Studio.

For each flower, you need:

- Print 1: 4 squares 3¼″ × 3¼″ and 4 squares 2½″ × 2½″ (blue outer bloom in top left block)

- Print 2: 4 squares 1¾″ × 1¾″ (blue inner bud in top left block)

- Print 3: 4 squares 3¼″ × 3¼″ and 4 squares 2½″ × 2½″ (green corner and star points)

- Print 4: 4 rectangles 1¾″ × 2″ (yellow in center of flower)

- Print 5: 1 square 2″ × 2″ (yellow checkerboard in center of flower)

- Background: 4 squares 3¼″ × 3¼″ and 8 squares 2½″ × 2½″

You will also need:

- Sashing: 40 rectangles 2½″ × 12½″

- Binding: 7 strips 2¼″ × the width of fabric

Even though I used scraps, there was a color plan for each block! In every block I used the same green for the corners and star points and the same two yellow fabrics for the flower center. The light fabric in each block is a tiny polka-dot print. For each flower, I used two prints in the same color family—one for the outer blooms and one for the inner bud.

Wishing Rings

Finished block: 7½ × 7½″   •   Finished quilt: 54″ × 69″

Wishing Rings, 54″ × 69″, made by Joyce Dean Gieszler, quilted by Cheryl Ferris, 2015

Materials

The feature project uses yardage for a consistent colorway. For a scrappier version, see Gears *(page 57).*

WHITE 3½ yards for the blocks and outer border

TURQUOISE PRINT: 2¾ yards for the blocks, inner border, and binding

BACKING: 3½ yards

BATTING: 62″ × 77″

This sweet quilt is perfect for gifts—a great snuggler size. My next one is planned with a pink-and-red floral fabric! It's a quick sew with diagonal corners that give it a uniqueness not found in many patterns. Instructions are included for binding unusual angles.

This was another time I was happy to have a bolt of white fabric on hand. My new favorite is a white-on-white fabric with a design that looks like stippling.

Cutting

WHITE

- Cut 1 rectangle 65″ × the width of fabric.

  On the vertical grain of fabric, subcut 4 rectangles 65″ × 5½″ and 72 rectangles 2″ × 5″.

- Cut 4 strips 8″ × the width of fabric.

  Subcut 17 squares 8″ × 8″.

  Subcut 4 squares 3½″ × 3½″.

- Cut 3 strips 2½″ × the width of fabric.

  Subcut 36 squares 2½″ × 2½″.

- Cut 5 strips 2″ × the width of fabric.

  Leave 1 strip whole. From the remaining strips, subcut 72 squares 2″ × 2″.

TURQUOISE PRINT

- Cut 1 rectangle 55″ × the width of fabric.

  On the vertical grain of fabric, subcut 4 rectangles 55″ × 3½″, 36 rectangles 2″ × 5″, and 36 squares 2½″ × 2½″.

- Cut 10 strips 2″ × the width of fabric.

  Leave 2 strips whole. From the remaining strips, subcut 144 squares 2″ × 2″.

- Cut 7 strips 2¼″ × the width of fabric for the binding.

Quilt Construction

Press all seams according to the arrows in the diagrams.

Strip Sets

Sew a 2″ white strip between 2 turquoise strips. Press the seams toward the turquoise fabrics. Cut 18 units 2″ wide from the strip set.

Make 1 strip set. Cut 18 units 2″ wide.

Stitch-and-Flip Rectangles

Note -

While it feels natural to press the seam allowance on these units toward the triangle, always press these seams toward the turquoise. This will make the seams nest beautifully when you assemble the block.

- -

1. Lightly draw a diagonal line from one corner to the opposite corner on all white 2″ × 2″ squares and turquoise 2″ × 2″ squares. With right sides together, place a white square on one corner of a 2″ × 5″ turquoise rectangle.

2. Sew directly on the line and trim the seam allowance to ¼″.

3. Press the seam allowance toward the turquoise.

4. Repeat with another white square on the opposite end of the rectangle. Make 36.

Make 36.

5. Repeat Steps 1–4 with 2 small turquoise squares and 1 white rectangle. Make 72.

Make 72.

Half-Square Triangles

Referring to Half-Square Triangles (page 60), use the 2½″ × 2½″ squares to make 72 half-square triangles. Square each to 2″ × 2″.

Block Construction

1. Lay out the half-square triangles, rectangle units, and center of the block as shown.

2. Sew them into rows and sew the rows together. Make 18.

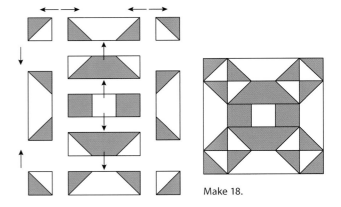

Make 18.

Quilt Assembly

1. Refer to the quilt center assembly diagram to lay out the quilt.

2. Sew the blocks together in rows, and then sew the rows together.

Quilt center assembly

Inner Border

1. Measure the length of the quilt through the center and cut 2 of the 3½″ turquoise strips to this measurement. Sew to the quilt sides, easing to fit as necessary. Press the seams toward the border. Repeat to apply the top and bottom borders to the quilt.

2. Draw a diagonal line from one corner to the opposite corner on the wrong side of the 3½″ × 3½″ white squares.

3. Place a 3½″ × 3½″ square on the corner of the quilt border. Stitch on the drawn line, being careful that the

diagonal is heading in the right direction. Trim the seam allowance to ¼″ and press the seam allowance toward the white. Repeat on all 4 corners.

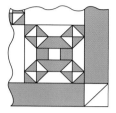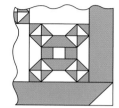

Outer Border

Refer to Inner Border, Step 1 to add the outer borders, using the 5½″ white strips. Wait to cut the diagonal angle on the final border until after the top is quilted.

Quilting and Finishing

1. Quilt and bind your quilt as desired. Cheryl Ferris quilted this top with an allover pantograph design called *Loopy Loops* by Kim Diamond of Sweet Dreams Design Studio.

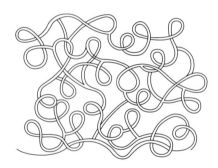

2. After quilting and trimming the quilt for binding, make a small mark 5¼″ from each corner of the quilt. Draw a faint diagonal line to connect the marks. Using the rotary cutter, cut on the diagonal line.

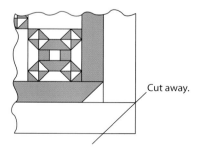

Cut away.

Binding

Treat this binding as you would any other with mitered corners. You just have 8 "corners" to miter instead of 4, and the angle turns out a bit differently.

1. Measure in ¼″ from each corner edge of the quilt. Mark the point with a pin or use a pencil to mark an *X*.

2. Lay out the binding loosely to make sure that a seam will not fall right at the corner.

3. Stitch to the pin or the penciled *X*. Backstitch, and remove the quilt from the machine.

4. Rotate the quilt and fold the binding straight up, and then fold it back down (just as you do with regular binding). Line up the binding with the next side to be sewn. Continue binding each corner in the same manner.

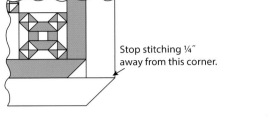

Stop stitching ¼″ away from this corner.

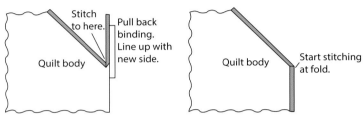

Stitch to here.

Pull back binding. Line up with new side.

Quilt body

Quilt body

Start stitching at fold.

Make your own quilt coloring page! Make an enlarged copy of this outline and then color it in to create your own color plan.

Gears, 54″ × 69″, made by Joyce Dean Gieszler, quilted by Cheryl Ferris, 2015

Gears

Simply changing the colors of the units in this quilt turns it into a fabulous quilt for any cycling enthusiast. The black and dark gray combine to look like the chain links of a bicycle! Use 1 yard of white, 2¾ yards of light gray, 1¼ yards of dark gray, and 1¼ yards of black. I had all the fabrics on hand for this quilt except the light gray background; I found that in the Christmas fabrics because it has snowflakes in the design. Cheryl Ferris quilted this scrappy version with an allover pantograph design called *Gear* by Kim Diamond of Sweet Dreams Quilt Studio.

QUILT making TECHNIQUES

To make your sewing a little easier, I've collected a few of my most-used techniques here, all in one spot.

I realize there are a lot of ways to sew different units, and those instructions could fill an entire book. For each technique, I focused on using just one method throughout the book to simplify the patterns. You may find other methods that work equally well for you or better. Use whatever technique works best for you.

I always recommend reading through an entire pattern before you start cutting to familiarize yourself with the sewing instructions. All yardage requirements are based on a 40˝ width of usable fabric.

If you are new to quilting, I recommend taking a class at your local quilt shop or searching online to learn more about basic rotary cutting and quiltmaking techniques. A good resource is C&T's Quiltmaking Basics: ctpub.com > Support > Quiltmaking Basics & Sewing Tips.

Stash Management

When to Buy New Yardage

I belong to an online group called Stashbusters that encourages members to use up their fabric stashes and complete their projects. The group has fabric swaps, stay-at-home retreats, and ongoing challenges. A "no buy" challenge, however, includes permission to buy background, borders, or backing. It seems like we frequently have fabrics that we can combine into the scrappy parts of the quilt but need permission to buy the larger pieces. I use this philosophy frequently when I'm trying to tame my stash. Of course, I usually go on a "no buy" challenge right after I've bought a lot of fabric!

In all seriousness, though, I buy fabric when I need it to complete a project, or when it needs to be perfect, or when I just plain fall in love with it. How else can I explain sixteen quilts coming out of my stash?

How I Store My Stash

My stash management techniques have been evolving over the years, and I anticipate that that will continue. I generally store fabrics together by color and genre, such as Civil War–era reproduction fabrics. I have a large storage system with nine cubbies, each containing a different color of fabric—green, red, yellow/orange, blue, gray, purple, pink, brown, and neutrals. Each cubby contains pieces that are smaller than 2 yards and larger than 4″×4″ squares.

I recently started saving smaller scraps of all colors in a tub because I'm on the fence about how small a scrap to keep! A friend uses small scraps to stuff dog beds for the local animal shelter, and I find that this solution has freed me up somewhat from my former compulsion to keep itty-bitty pieces.

I do not precut any sizes or shapes unless I have a specific project in mind. For example, I found a pattern that contained 1,300 half-square triangles and knew I wanted it to be really scrappy. Every time I used a fabric, I cut a 2½″ strip from some of the scraps (anywhere from 6″ to 20″). I put all of those aside in a tub until I had enough lights and darks to start making the units. For the most part, however, bright fabrics are in one spot and Civil War–era reproduction fabrics in another.

I store large pieces of fabric in stacks on a bookshelf so they're easy to see and use. I put projects in tubs, with fabrics and drawings or a pattern, until I'm ready to sew them. Even if I have set aside a fabric for a particular project, though, it is still fair game to use in any quilt. To my mind it's easier to replace fabric for a future project than it is to find the perfect fabric for a current one.

Sewing Techniques

Clipping Bulky Seam Allowances

Sometimes the intersection of quilt blocks gets very bulky, or I find that I've pressed incorrectly when sewing the blocks. If that happens, I clip on each side of that intersection and press the center seams open to reduce the bulk. The clips are approximately ¼″ away from each side of a seam intersection. For example, *Spinning Triangles* (page 12) has a lot of small pieces that may create bulky intersections. If you find that you don't like the way the pieces come together, feel free to use this clipping technique to minimize the bulk so it is less evident on the front of the quilt.

Half-Square Triangles

1. With right sides together, pair 2 squares. Lightly draw a diagonal line from one corner to the opposite corner on the wrong side of the lighter square.

2. Sew a scant ¼″ seam on each side of the line.

3. Cut on the drawn line.

4. Press toward the darker fabric.

5. Trim to the size listed in the pattern.

Quarter-Square Triangles

1. Make the number of half-square triangles specified in the pattern instructions.

2. Pair the half-square triangles according to the pattern instructions. For example, in *What's Up* (page 34), you would pair 1 white/red half-square triangle with 1 white/blue half-square triangle. Draw a diagonal line perpendicular to the seam on the wrong side of a half-square triangle.

3. Layer the 2 half-square triangles, right sides together, with the dark colors opposite each other. If you pressed the seams of the half-square triangles toward the darker fabrics, your seams should nest together.

4. Sew a scant ¼″ seam on each side of the line. Cut apart on the diagonal line.

5. Open and press the seams to one side. This makes 2 quarter-square triangles.

Specialty Binding

Sometimes a quilt just calls for binding that is two different colors on the front side of the quilt. Two quilts in this book utilize this style of binding. For example, *Snowbirds* (page 40) uses 4 strips of aqua fabric and 4 strips of blue fabric. To make the fabrics miter at the corners of the quilt, follow these instructions.

1. Join the 2¼˝ strips of binding fabric with diagonal seams. To make a diagonal seam, place 2 strips right sides together, with 1 strip perpendicular to the other. Sew a diagonal line from corner to corner, checking to ensure the seam creates 1 long length of binding before trimming the seam allowance to ¼˝. Press all seam allowances open. In the case of *College Bound* (page 45), you would sew the 4 green strips together and the 4 yellow strips together.

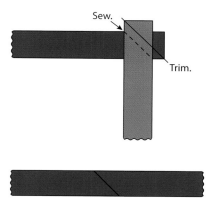

2. Fold the binding strips in half with wrong sides together. Press, being careful not to stretch the binding.

3. On the back of the quilt, measure ¼˝ in from the corner in each direction and mark with a pin. Repeat for all 4 corners.

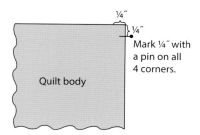

4. Start with the first color of binding at the upper right corner of the quilt (corner 1). Extend the binding approximately 6˝ from the corner and start stitching ¼˝ from the top edge of the quilt. Be sure to backstitch to secure. When you reach the next corner (corner 2), turn the corner just as you would with a traditional binding.

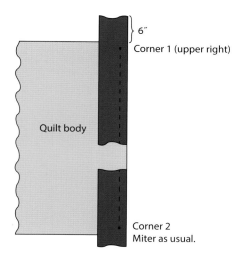

5. When you reach the next corner (corner 3), where the 2 colors will join, stop stitching ¼˝ from the corner. Backstitch, and remove the quilt from the machine. Trim the tail of the binding to approximately 6˝ beyond the backstitching.

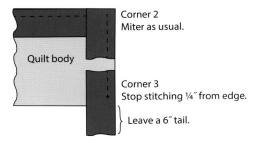

Corner 2
Miter as usual.

Quilt body

Corner 3
Stop stitching ¼˝ from edge.

Leave a 6˝ tail.

6. Starting at corner 3, repeat Steps 3 and 4 with the second color of binding, being careful not to catch the first binding in the stitching.

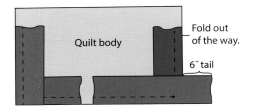

Quilt body

Fold out of the way.

6˝ tail

7. Corners 1 and 3 should have loose tails. Turn the quilt so the first set of loose tails is in the lower right-hand corner.

8. Pull the vertical binding tail to the right side, forming a 45° angle. Pull the horizontal binding to the right side and align on top of the vertical binding tail.

9. Measure the binding from the fold to the stitching line. Mine was ⅞˝ using 2¼˝ binding strips. Lightly draw a square of that same measurement onto the binding strip. Draw an *X* in the square.

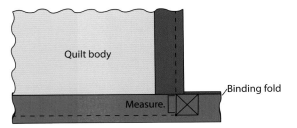

Quilt body

Measure.

Binding fold

10. Pin the binding ends together to hold them in place. Pull the quilt body out of the way and stitch on the left of the *X*, backstitching at the beginning and end of the seam. Once you are sure that the binding tails have stayed aligned, trim the seam allowance to ¼˝.

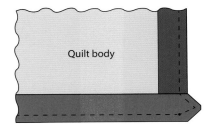

Quilt body

11. Repeat Steps 8–10 on the other corner with loose tails.

12. Bring the folded edge of the binding to the quilt back to cover the machine stitches. The 2-color corners will already be mitered on both sides of the quilt! Blindstitch the long folded edges to the quilt backing.

About the Author

Photo by Katie Gieszler

Joyce's lifelong love affair with sewing began when she was four years old. She told her mother she knew why the sewing machine was called a Singer—because it hummed! She took sewing in home economics, but didn't really begin to love sewing clothes until she was in her early twenties. Joyce began her sewing career tailoring men's suits in the Portland, Oregon, area.

After a move to Waco, Texas, she found a quilt shop inside a converted carriage house. It was love at first sight! Several moves (California and Florida) and two children later, Joyce's love affair with quilts was firmly planted.

For Joyce, among the greatest joys of quiltmaking are helping students recognize their talent and instilling in them a love of quilting. Her favorite times are when students (of any age) insist that they cannot be successful. The more skeptical they are, the better. Joyce hasn't met a student yet who couldn't be successful given enough different ways to sew the same unit.

Joyce has been teaching quilting for more than fifteen years and designing quilt patterns for nearly as long. She began teaching by volunteering at a local alternative school where she taught teen moms to make quilts for their babies. Joyce was honored to be the featured quilter in her adopted hometown of Hillsboro, Oregon, in 2010 and again in 2015. Joyce and her husband, Mike, are the proud parents of two adult children and a lovely daughter-in-law.

This is Joyce's second book. The first, *Then and Now Quilts,* was published in 2014. If you'd like to keep up with Joyce's current design projects, you can find her on her blog at www.quilterchickdesigns.com or her Quilterchick Designs Facebook page.

Resources

Quilters

AnnMarie Cowley
Hillsboro, Oregon
runandsewuilts.wordpress.com

Cheryl Ferris
Hillsboro, Oregon
creativeheartsquilting.com

Want even more creative content?

Make it, snap it, share it *using* *#ctpublishing*